A NEW Manc Alphabet

CW00349867

an illustrated collection
of new poetry

A New Manchester Alphabet was devised by Louise Clennell and Iris Feindt.

A New Manchester Alphabet was edited by Jean Sprackland.

A New Manchester Alphabet was art directed by Ian Whadcock.

Published by The Manchester Writing School
Department of English
Manchester Metropolitan University

Copyright © 2015

First edition published in December 2015

All rights reserved. No part of this publication may be reproduced, stored in a retrieval system, or be transmitted in any form, or by any means, electronic, photocopying or otherwise, without prior written permission of the publisher. The copyright of each poem remains with the author; the copyright for each illustration remains with the artist; Manchester Metropolitan University owns copyright of the anthology as a composite work.

Cover image by Ian McCullough.

Designed by Anna Evans and Jo Phillips, The Design Studio, Marketing, Communications and Development, Manchester Metropolitan University.

A Manchester Alphabet was written and illustrated by Roger Oldham (1871-1916). It was published in Manchester by John Heywood in 1906.

Printed and bound in England by MMU Print Services.

ISBN 978-1-910029-11-4

A New Manchester Alphabet: Introduction

In 1906 Roger Oldham, a member of the Manchester Society of Architects, wrote and illustrated a small booklet called *A Manchester Alphabet*. The *Alphabet* takes us on a journey around Edwardian Manchester from Ancoats to the (Bellevue) Zoo, with a wit and charm that appeals to adults and children alike.

Fast forward to 2014, and a copy of the original booklet is found on the shelves at Manchester Metropolitan University's Special Collections, home to the Library of the Manchester Society of Architects. Leafing through its pages it is clear that many of the places depicted by Roger Oldham remain; some have changed beyond recognition, others are exactly as they were all those years ago. To coincide with the 150th anniversary of the Manchester Society of Architects in 2015, we decided to re-visit the *Alphabet* and take it into the present day.

A New Manchester Alphabet is a snapshot of Manchester in 2015: illustrated by students from the Manchester School of Art and written by students from The Manchester Writing School at Manchester Metropolitan University. This collaboration of illustrators and writers takes us on a brand new journey: from Afflecks, via New Islington, to Ziferblat. When you get to the end, take a minute to ponder. Then, get ready to venture into the past and explore Roger Oldham's *Manchester Alphabet*. Imagine what it might have been like, all those years ago, and dream up your own Manchester Alphabet.

The Manchester Writing School, the Manchester School of Art and MMU Special Collections are delighted to present *A New Manchester Alphabet*.

A for Afflecks

The place to unearth that Gothic dress
to impress your countercultural friends,
or something from the 60s for your mam:

Afflecks, a kind of ecofriendly Debenhams.
Find here a classic by Led Zeppelin
on vinyl, get its cover inked on your skin

while tourists gawk, goading themselves on
towards their virgin tattoos, toetapping to
the Whole Lotta Love you bought your dad.

AFFLECKS
DISCO
T-REX
ZOMBIE

B for Beetham Tower

To the hiker thirty miles away on Frodsham Hill
it's a stake in the ground, says "here lies a city
of smokeless stacks and post-Satanic mills,"
though nothing else mars his view of the moors.

Driving in on the M56 the glass of its 47th floor
reflects the sunset as far out as Altrincham,
the long stretch of Princess Road it's a guiding star
until, over Mancunian Way, it's the Holy Grail.

Tourists on Deansgate get vertigo peering to see
what it is that, in strong winds, hums in a key of B.

revolution

C for Cathedral

A bronze St George frees the Dragon of Our Piety,
who has two sides as piety always does:
one an insister on rites, an adherent to books,
one a less famous sincerity.
Fresh from centuries of lonely sobriety
he no longer swallows wine to light it up,
drinks in Evensong, the stained-glass blood drops
the life-affirming woodwork, and friendly society;
where walls are blasted down then built back up,
and some left broken down, and myths are broken down.

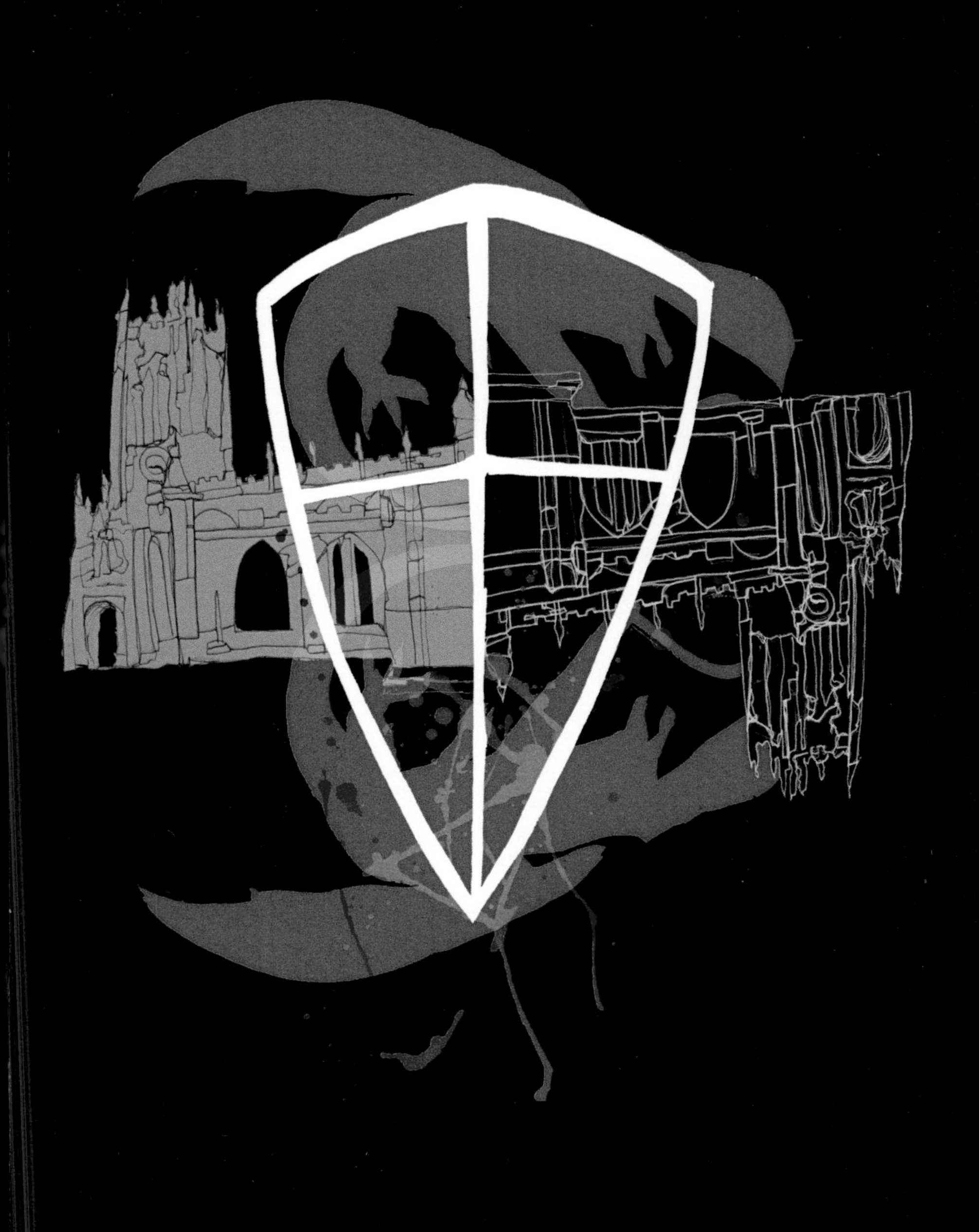

for Didsbury

We are part of it: a layout
of loose ends, dead ends,

split ends. Didsbury DNA
is our gene map of roads,

strands of tall houses,
replicating one another,

the nuclei of front doors,
our red brick walls.

All derivative
of our lives, our sweat

and layered just as you'd expect.

LIBRARY
FOLK
BARBER

E for Etihad Stadium

An Arabic word meaning union for a game that divides a city.
A name about sponsors with a history still to be made
and with one to live up to, old names still alive inside –
Colin Bell, Kippax, the Scoreboard End.
So what does Etihad Stadium mean to you?
The home of Manchester's Citizens, the lads in sky blue.

F for Alex Ferguson

Alex Ferguson, poet-manager of Manchester United,

a mentor of few words, yet elegant foot play,

welded in steel, chiselled to grit,

tactician with a leopard's stealth,

laureate of the city's dreams,

gambler on the pitch – mind the watch.

Don't look at the time. Keep the opposition

under pressure. That's a little trick.

G for Graphene

Perhaps before their pencil, in that building
it was in me that flat form carbon atom;
hexagonally honeycombed.
Undiscovered and waiting.
And before that did it come from a star?
Maybe it was once inside you.
You are a study in graphene;
cleaved graphite, harder than diamond,
stronger than steel. Exceptional.
Now nanotube rolls push us forward.

H for Hospitality

Manchester folk will put you up,

put up with your strange ways.

If drenched by rainy days,

we've lots of warmth to share.

So strike a conversation up

at bus stop, food shop, local pub.

Or ask us for directions and

we'll almost take you there!

for Ice Plant

It's the first days of summer in a new millennium,
Victoria is on the throne, and down Blossom Street
they're loading ice onto the cart of an Italian

ice cream seller. The ironshod wheels creak
as the ice is shoveled out of its canvas sack
into barrels where he stores his cold vanilla treats

safe from the sulfur-yellowed sun. It's still dark
outside the Ice Plant, the cobbles slippy with dew,
as he pays for the ice and trundles off with his cart

at a rattle, dreaming that one day sky will be blue.

J for Jewish Museum

Come in. See the Torah rescued from the Nazis' grip,
take in all you can about this faith full of ancient ritual.
Now climb the stairs as countless women used to do,
meet Cheena Livshin. Say a prayer for her.
Pray for her as she stays in Cheetham Hill to have her boy,
for her man who goes to make their new home –
drowns on the Titanic.
Pray for the countless women whose wigs she made.
Raise your voices. Pray for all the Cheena Livshins.

K for Karl Marx

Chetham's shelves concede
tome after tome of black cursive,
until pages shift and blur

the writing into a silhouette
of terraces, flanked on three sides
by factories, seventy feet tall or more.

A line of workers moves beneath
grey smoke that pitches to black
stains for clouds. In the yard, puddles

glisten like some filth syphoned up
from the underworld. No sunlight
to ever melt them from the shadows.

And it is then that he realizes
what Engels has given him.
He picks up his own pen and writes.

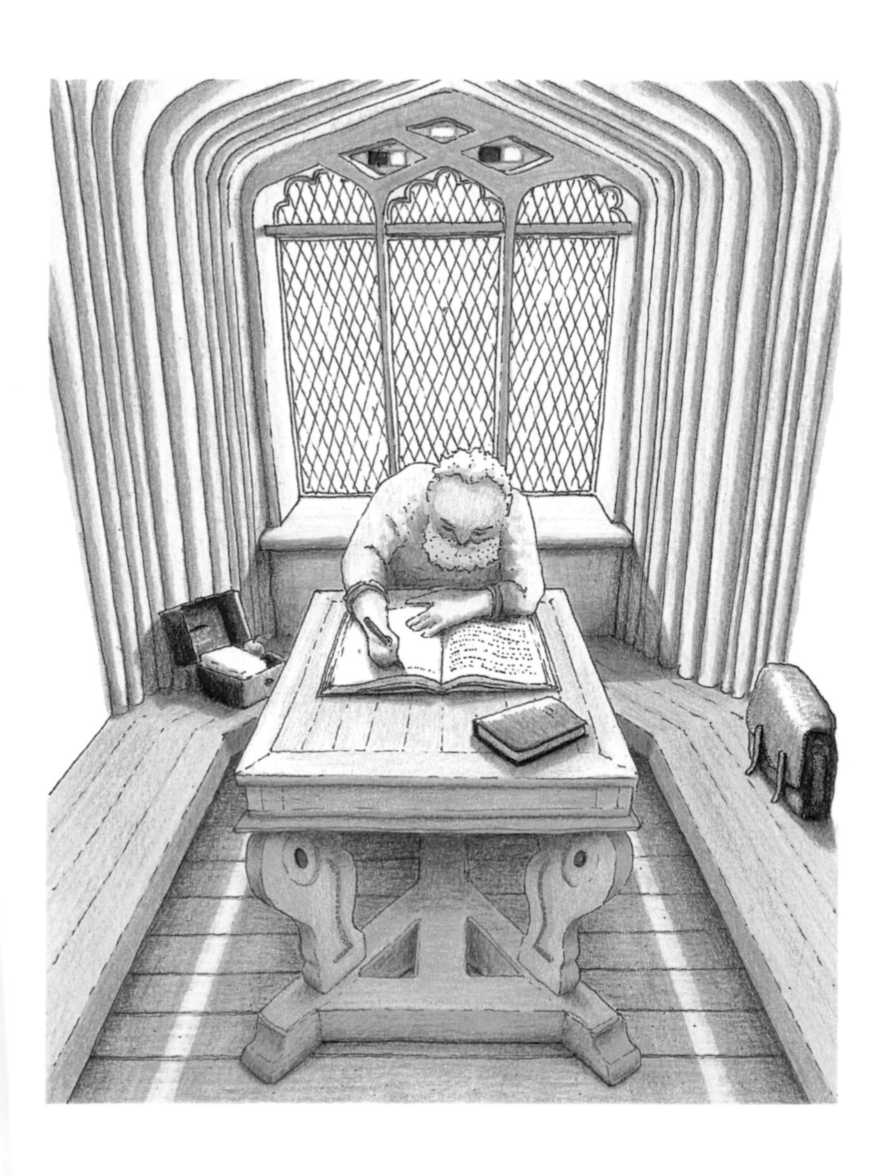

L for Libraries

We'll start at the Portico with Captain Cook – he will show the way;
we'll watch Victorian travellers explore the empires of Mosley Street,

then – fortified by new-found knowledge – walk to John Rylands to find
our spiritual guide. Caxton may fulfill our needs or, failing that, *Ulysses*.

Let's browse all the books we choose and sunbathe with their pages
under clearstorey windows – we'll see truer there. Revived,

we'll head to Chetham's, hold our hush and listen, crouching with its ghost
cats, mouse for knowledge in manuscripts and catch Donne by the tail.

Ready, we will go to the Central Library for our tryst among its columns.
Each reader Manchester can muster will borrow each book; on the count

of one, two, three – we'll open the volumes wide, see ideas unpeel from pages,
watch words turn birds, circling the city as we learn to hatch fresh thoughts.

Portico Library
Chetham's Library
John Ryland's Library
Manchester Central Library
53.478056°N
2.244722°W
53.480321°N
2.2487°W
53.2912°N
2.1439.W
1899
1890
1653
17/07/193
Sandstone
manuscripts
Victorian
Neo-Gothic
1930
1421

for Music

Johnny go *Hit it* on the Oxford Road
Moss Side messing to all saintly à la mode

Johnny opened doors, strummed onto the scene
bit short of technique, you know what I mean

but Johnny go *Blow it* for variety dance
when Hallé came knocking he rocked up to chance

and Johnny go *Play it;* that smooth saxophone
caught Barbarolli and those roses of stone

they all found their music as Manchester strode
thanks to Johnny who *Hit it* on the Oxford Road

JOHNNY ROADHOUSE MUSIC

for New Islington

At this slow convergence

of nestled treasure and newbuild –

the curated among the resurgent –

of dazzling sunlight raining down

upon woven reaches of silver water

out of acres of lately cleared sky,

onto mallards, pairings of regal swans,

wintering geese and narrowboats tethered

to mooring rings –

to this the migrant comes.

O for Roger Oldham

Roger Oldham came from Lincoln but learnt literacy
in Manchester, one street after another spilling
into idiom and illustration. A tall man, Oldham Street
carries his name but not his crown, as it should
be, of course, because no one owns what belongs
to the crowd. As Roger had it, boulevard, perpendicular,
heart of the Northern Quarter and Manchester Methodism,
you can't so much get lost here as fan out at either
end: south into fountain, concrete, wheel, and tram;
north, toward hill, moor, promontory, and sky.

P for Proper Tea

Tea's a ceremony here –
comes with timer and glass jug.
Pull up a chair, chat
with the Minor Canon
who sips Tippy Earl Grey,
keeps an eye on the shop.

Q for Quay Street

Legacy of freight: a road named
and paved for a great oily chain
of river that spewed iron, pulleys
cogs and gears, until the last hissing
stone was anchored into place.

8–100
00 Quay

for Ernest Rutherford

e h

Ma t f

p o

p un iv

i er se ic

ng t r

h b

e f a

for Suffragettes

Deeds not words came the battle cry,

paint was thrown, windows smashed, letters burned, trains crashed.

Here, for Emmeline three women struck; the attendant said '*they ran amok*.'

Annie, Lily and Evelyn fought the fight for a basic right,

were caught with hammers in their hands

in Manchester that April night, one hundred years ago.

Broken art for broken promises, they knew the price to pay –

so would I dare to raise my hand, to take a turn to make a stand

to brave the feeds and tubes and pain,

like Annie, Lily and Evelyn…

DEEDS NOT WORDS
VOTES FOR WOMEN
FREE TRADE HALL
MANCHESTER ART GALLERY
HRH
HRH
W.S.P.U
DEEDS NOT WORDS
WSPU
V

T for Alan Turing

If I were Alan Turing, I'd choose too
to sit in Sackville Gardens, watch couples
strolling free, enjoy the changing view
of what passes here for greenery,
and see slowly bloom the LGBT scene.

And if I sit beside him long enough,
keep still enough, stay silent as posterity,
might not then his heart of bronze forgive
those who forged his martyrdom,
and might he share his apple with me?

ANAL

for Umbrella

A gust thrust them skyward
and they were sailing on air.
Higher and higher they rose until
they landed on a huge soft cloud.
Look up and you'll see them
laughing at us getting wet – all those
big black stretched-out smiles.

V for Victoria Baths

Enough tiled temples already
for gods and alcohol: this shrine's
just for water, its shimmer and splash,
its cleansing buoyancy.
Swing back the cubicle doors,
break the surface, breathe,
immerse yourself in another time.

W for The Whitworth

The red-brick welcome hasn't changed;
northern warmth still guides you in.
The art is world-class, varied, bold,
but there's more space to breathe now
so take your time.

New glass walls embrace the park.
The café looks out into trees,
so let the green refresh your eyes
before a second look around.
You'll feel restored.

for Xmas Markets

Take the banter of the city. Wrap it
in tissue paper (the kind that crunches
like fresh snow) and pop it into
a velveteen box, redder than Santa's hat.
Then sprinkle in some sparkle
before tying it all up with golden ribbon.
And that's your Manchester Xmas Market –
a bargain at £7.99. Three for twenty
to you, luv. But don't tell anyone.

BEER
meats
cheeses

Y for Yang Sing

She who pours tea
for her elders
will see a thousand moons.

He who takes
the last prawn dumpling
without asking
if anyone else wants it,
will see stars.

羊
YANG SING
城

for Ziferblat

Zifferblatt, n. (Russian and German) clock face

Here are the clock hands' constellations:

Twelve o'clock is the Shut Eye.
Half six is Pursed Lips.
And these other positions
are the juggled Hands of the Mime.

They endlessly shape
a ball of empty space,
making something from nothing.
Time out of time.

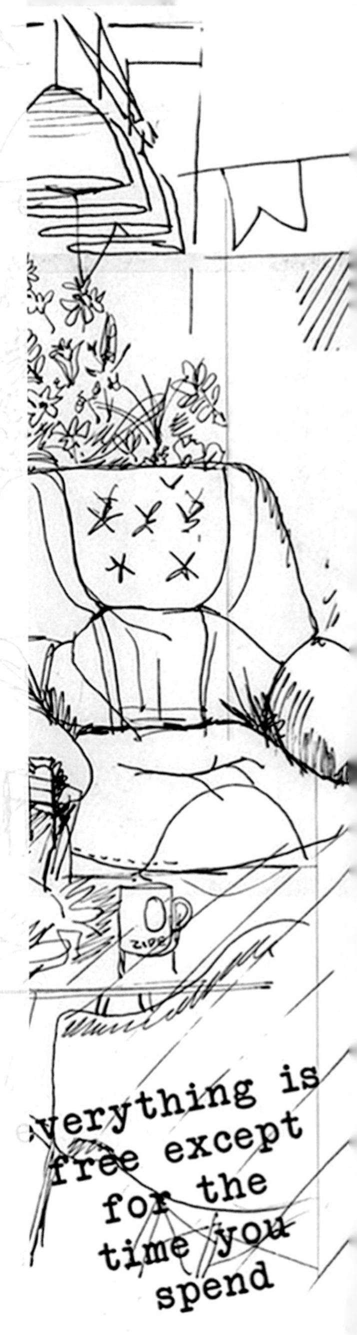

Welcome to
Ziferblat
Help yourself to our
goodies but be fair
to others in our space
ZIFERBLAT

A words: Andy Hickmott
image: Julia Gallego

B words: Andy Hickmott
image: Antony Cross

C words: Merrie Williams
image: Gemma Kelly

D words: Elisabeth Sennitt Clough
image: Susie Purvis

E words: Vicki Stannard
image: Dominika Wroblewska

F words: Maggie Mackay
image: Peter McEwan

G words: Sue Finch
image: Liam Rotheram

H words: Merrie Williams
image: Elsa Frere

I words: Andy Hickmott
image: Dominika Wroblewska

J words: Hilary Robinson
image: Kate Patterson

K words: Elisabeth Sennitt Clough
image: Peter McEwan

L words: Georgi Gill
image: Rebecca Ritchie

M words: Robert Harper
image: Hannah Marchant

N words: Andy Hickmott
image: Eva Akësson

O words: Nikolai Duffy
image: Katie Williams

P words: Hilary Robinson
image: Kate Patterson

Q words: Elisabeth Sennitt Clough
image: Dominika Wroblewska

R words: Georgi Gill
image: Liam Rotheram

S words: Valerie Bence
image: Catherine Pearl

T words: Andy Hickmott
image: Antony Cross

U words: Ian Humphreys
image: Elsa Frere

V words: Andrew Rudd
image: Esme Mackey

W words: Natalie Burdett
image: Peter McEwan

X words: Ian Humphreys
image: Susie Purvis

Y words: Ian Humphreys
image: Julia Gallego

Z words: Martin Kratz
image: Cherie Jerrard

M. S. A. Club Room.

with the author's compliments.

A fellow of the Institute.
who joins the M.S.A.
Can get this club & things to boot.
with nothing more to pay.

MANCHESTER SOCIETY
OF ARCHITECTS.

1/- NET.

A MANCHESTER ALPHABET

WRITTEN & DRAWN BY ROGER OLDHAM

JOHN HEYWOOD LTD · DEANSGATE & RIDGEFIELD MANCHESTER · & LAMBS · CONDUIT ST LONDON W.C.

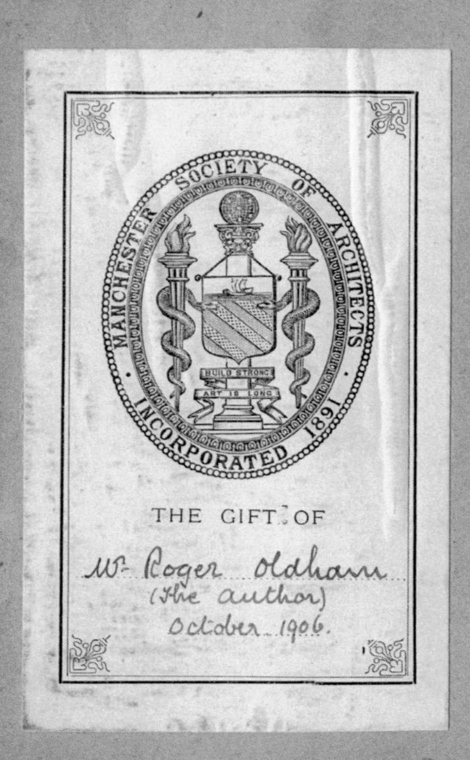
MANCHESTER SOCIETY OF ARCHITECTS
INCORPORATED 1891
BUILD STRONG
ART IS LONG
THE GIFT OF
Mr Roger Oldham
(The author)
October 1906.

FOREWORD·

SOME·DO·NOT·THINK·THESE
POEMS·GOOD·AH·WELL
I·NEVER·THOUGHT·THEY
WOULD·IN·FACT·I·DONT
KNOW·WHICH·THE·WORSE
IS·THE·TASTE·THE·GRAMMAR
OR·THE·VERSES· R·O·

A for ANCOATS

A dreary place is Ancoats,
'Tis full of smoke and fogs,
The lasses wear shawls on their heads
Their feet are shod with clogs.
'Tis really not a pleasant place
Upon a rainy day ;
We have to start with Ancoats tho',
For Ancoats starts with A.

CLOGGER
R·O

B for BOWDON

The men who sleep in Bowdon
In Manchester by day are,
They travel by the C.L.C.
Or M.S.J. & A.R.

RO

C for CHORLTON

Chorlton's in the suburbs,
The Houses there have gates,
And people come in winter time,
If frosty, with their skates.

R.O

D for DALTON

John Dalton lived in Manchester
A hundred years ago,
A famous scientific man
As all the world doth know.
He's fishing now in our Town Hall
In stagnant H_2O.

R·O

E for EXCHANGE

The Royal Exchange has a very big floor
But it's not big enough, so they open the door
And come out in the street, do merchants galore.

MANCHESTER · ROYAL · EXCHANGE
EXTENDED
REBUILT
R.O

F for FRESCO

Historical scenes of Manchester town
Were painted in fresco by Ford Madox Brown.
A fresco is something that can't run away
It's stuck on the plaster for ever and aye.

SIZE
R.O

G for "GUARDIAN"

"The Guardian" is a candid friend
And guide to sundry persons,
It compliments the very good
And scarifies the worse 'uns.

MANCHESTER GUARDIAN·
R·O.

H for HEATON PARK

Let children come
From dreary slum
And din of dusty highways,
And once a week
Play hide and seek
In nature's leafy by-ways.

RO

I for IRWELL

I is for IRWELL
for IRK
and for INK,

But none of these Liquids
Is wholesome to drink.

R·O

J for JOULE

Just peep inside the Town Hall door
And there you will espy
An old man in his dressing gown
Who looks with stony eye
At something he holds in his hand,
I do not quite know why.

JOULE
R.O

K for KING STREET

There's King Street
And there's King Street South
And also King Street West,
They each of them begin with K,
I know which I like best—
The one in which the cake shop is—
* * * * *
Let's go inside and rest.

CAKES
RO

L for LORD MAYOR

The Lord Mayor is a lovely sight
All in his coat of red,
A golden chain about his neck,
A big hat on his head ;
He entertains the city's guests
And sees that they are fed.

STUDIO
R.O.

M for MOTOR CAR

The face and pace of Manchester
Have many changes seen,
From the grass of Angel Meadow
And the blades of Ardwick Green ;
From the Pack Horse and the Pillion
And " the ancient Seven Stars,"
To the modern mammoth Midland
And the monstrous Motor Cars.

AND
SONS.
TEA & COFFE
THOS T
CHEES
R.O.

N

Now these monstrous Motor Cars,
The product of the age,
(As has only just been mentioned
On the last preceding page)
Have a letter put behind them
To signify to men
The place which they belong to,
Thus :—Manchester is N.

N 8597
R.O.

O for OWL

The Grammar School Owl,
That very wise fowl,
Was the crest of the pious Hugh Oldham,
Who made it a rule
When he founded the School
That the boys should do always what's
told 'em.

R.O
O.M

P for PICTURE GALLERY

Go up some steps in Mosley Street
And through a sculpture hall,
Climb up some further flights of steps,
And thro' a turnstile crawl,
At last behold the pictures,
Hung up on every wall.

R.O

Q for De QUINCEY

De Quincey once lived at a place called
Greenhey
Which *was* a green place in T. Quincey's
day.

T Q
ARABIAN NIGHTS.
MRS BAR-BAULD
R.O.

R for ROBERT

This monument so stately
To the late Sir Robert Peel,
Is the guardian of our traffic
And the public commonweal.

R·O

S for SHUDEHILL

Heaps of oranges and apples,
Piles of "tates" and curly greens,
Bananas, sprouts, and artichokes,
Late peas and early beans,
Inside a great glass market
Is what Shudehill really means.

R·O

T for TRAMS

The Tram Cars glide about the streets
As if they were alive,
And men and women fight for seats
Each night at half past five.

R.O.

U for UMPIRE

They keep men at Old Trafford
In snowy raiment clad,
To tell men when they are run out
And if the light is bad.

R.O.

V for VICTORIA

A model of nobility
To all of every station,
Victoria the well-beloved
The mother of the nation.

R·O

W for WHIT-WEEK WALK

The scholars' walk in Manchester
Is quite a pretty sight,
The boys all have their faces washed,
Their boots with blacking bright,
The girls all have their hair in curl,
Their dresses spotless white.

R.O.

X for EXODUS

Each Saturday at 1 o'clock
The people leave the town en bloc,
But if you wait till 10 to 2
You'll only see a very few.

BATHS
PRINCES
OUTING CLUB
R.O

Y for YARN

To business men in Manchester
The Yarn is daily bread,
They talk of hanks and mules and counts,
And throstle-frames and thread,
As did their grandsires long ago
Who now, of course, are dead.

R.O.

Z for ZOO

Belle Vue it is true
Is a very good Zoo,
Brass bands and rip-raps
And set pieces too,
Are part of the programme
At Manchester Zoo.

R.O.